# From Advent to Christ the King

## Following the Liturgical Calendar

### Reproducible Handouts for Junior High

Active Learning for Catholic Teens

Hi-Time✳Pflaum

Dayton, Ohio

From Advent to Christ the King

Following the Liturgical Calendar

Active Learning for Catholic Teens

Reproducible Handouts for Junior High

Activities by Nancy Regensburger
Nancy holds a master's degree in Theological Studies, with a major in biblical studies from St. John's Provincial Seminary, Plymouth, MI. She has written study materials for religious publishers for more than a decade. Nancy lives with her husband in Michigan, has two grown children and four grandchildren.

*Cover by Larissa Thompson*

*Interior Design by Linda Becker*

Crossword puzzles generated using Crossword Studio by Nordic Software™, with content and images provided by Hi-Time✳Pflaum.

ISBN: 0-937997-90-0

# Contents

## Notes to Teacher

# Cycles of My Life

Name_____

This poem from the Old Testament book of Ecclesiastes shows the heights and depths of human life. Just as the seasons of the years spiral forward with regularity, so each of our lives has a rhythm, and events come at appointed times. If we are in tune with the rhythm, we can choose proper activities for the various times in the cycles.

*For everything there is a season,
and a time for every matter under heaven:
a time to be born, and a time to die;
a time to plant, and a time to pluck up what is planted;
a time to kill, and a time to heal;
a time to break down, and a time to build up;
a time to weep, and a time to laugh;
a time to mourn, and a time to dance;
a time to throw away stones, and a time to gather stones together;
a time to embrace, and a time to refrain from embracing;
a time to seek, and a time to lose;
a time to keep, and a time to throw away;
a time to tear, and a time to sew;
a time to keep silence, and a time to speak;
a time to love, and a time to hate;
a time for war, and a time for peace.
Ecclesiastes 3:1-8*

1. Circle a phrase from this Scripture that describes this present time in your own life.

2. Choose a name for this period of your life. When did it begin? When might it end?

_____

_____

3. What activities fill your days now?

_____

_____

4. How do you feel physically? emotionally? spiritually?

_____

_____

5. Who are the people most important to you at this point in your life?

_____     _____     _____

_____     _____     _____

# Birth, Growth, Death, Rebirth

Name_____

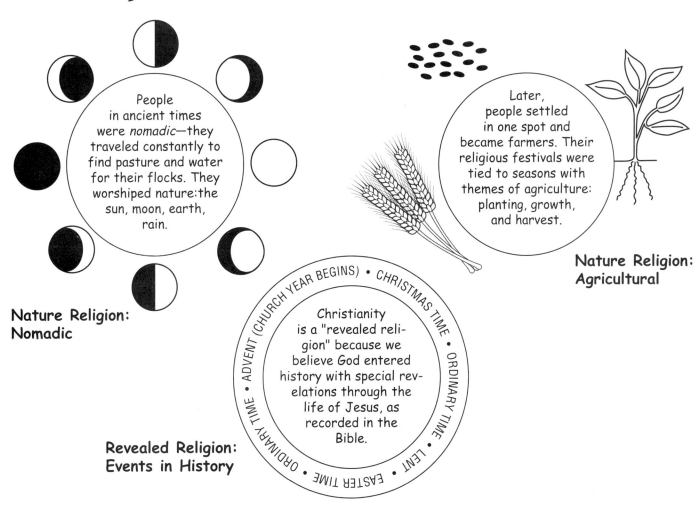

People in ancient times were *nomadic*—they traveled constantly to find pasture and water for their flocks. They worshiped nature: the sun, moon, earth, rain.

**Nature Religion: Nomadic**

Later, people settled in one spot and became farmers. Their religious festivals were tied to seasons with themes of agriculture: planting, growth, and harvest.

**Nature Religion: Agricultural**

ADVENT (CHURCH YEAR BEGINS) • CHRISTMAS TIME • ORDINARY TIME • LENT • EASTER TIME • ORDINARY TIME •

Christianity is a "revealed religion" because we believe God entered history with special revelations through the life of Jesus, as recorded in the Bible.

**Revealed Religion: Events in History**

Belief in the cycle of life (birth, growth, death, rebirth) is a core truth in all three religion types. It refers not just to resurrection at the end of physical life but to all the little deaths and rebirths within our lives while on earth.

## Reflection

Identify one holiday (holy day) from the liturgical year and write a short story of something good that happened to you at that time. What is the original story of the holiday? Does your story reflect the spirit of the original story? Explain.

_____

_____

_____

_____

*If you need more room, use another sheet of paper.*

# How We Celebrate Our Year

Name_____

## The Liturgical Seasons

For Catholics and other Christians, the life of Jesus and the early Church overlays the calendar and adds a spiritual dimension to the cycle of each year. These are the seasons of the year and a short explanation of each.

| | |
|---|---|
| Advent | We prepare for the coming of Christ. |
| Christmastime | We celebrate the birth and baptism of Jesus. |
| Lent | We recall the suffering and death of Jesus. |
| Triduum | Begins with Holy Thursday Mass and ends on Easter evening. |
| Eastertime | We celebrate Jesus' victory over death. |
| Ordinary Time | Two periods: one is between Christmastime and Lent; the other is after Eastertime until the beginning of Advent. |

The colors used during the seasons and on special feasts signify particular themes. The priests' vestments, the banners, and other liturgical enhancements change to denote the season. The most frequently used colors are white, violet (or purple), red, and green. White signifies innocence, purity, and joy. Violet, or purple, represents penitence and preparation. Red is for sacrifice and the Holy Spirit. Green stands for hope and spiritual growth.

Directions: Using the liturgical color and the clue, fill in the name of the appropriate season or feast.

| Color | Clue | Season or Feast |
|---|---|---|
| 1. red | Holy Spirit | |
| 2. white | gold, frankincense, myrrh | |
| 3. violet | wreath with candles | |
| 4. white | Baptism | |
| 5. white | Last Supper | |
| 6. red | tree branches | |
| 7. white | empty tomb | |
| 8. white | role models | |
| 9. violet | ashes | |
| 10. red | Golgotha | |

# Immaculate Conception
## December 8

Name_____

The feast of the Immaculate Conception is a celebration of Mary's being free from original sin at birth and from every other sin during her life. This favor was given to her as a special grace by God. The Gospel of Luke has a beautiful poem, sung by Mary, when she tells her cousin Elizabeth she is to give birth. Elizabeth tells Mary she is blessed among women.

Read Mary's Song of Praise in Luke 1:46-55, then list in the left column all who will experience God's mercy, and in the right, those who will be turned away.

**God's Mercy**

_____

_____

_____

**Turned Away**

_____

_____

_____

In which category is Mary? (See Luke 1:48.)

_____

Considering the description in Mary's Song, give an example of a group today who you think might receive God's mercy. Explain.

_____

_____

Do you think you are one of God's lowly servants or a proud, rich ruler? Why?

_____

_____

# Our Lady of Guadalupe
## December 12

Name_____

In a great church in Mexico City there hangs a *tilma* (cloak) made of cactus cloth. That type of cloth seldom lasts more than twenty years, but this one has lasted for centuries. The cloak belonged to Juan Diego, who was an Aztec—one of the native people of Mexico. In 1531, at Guadalupe, Mary appeared to him. She was dressed as an Aztec princess, with dark skin and hair. Around her waist she wore a sash that was worn by pregnant women at that time.

Mary spoke kindly to Juan and asked that a church be built on the site. When he told the bishops, they didn't believe him. As a sign, Mary guided Juan to a spot where wild roses were blooming—in the middle of winter. Juan gathered the roses under the tilma to show the bishops. When he opened his cloak the bishops saw an image of Mary on the inside of the tilma!

A few years earlier, the Spanish explorer, Hernando Cortez, had made contact with the Aztec people and introduced them to Christianity. The Spanish, however, did not live their religion as Christians because they treated the Aztecs cruelly. Mary's appearance as an Aztec was a rebuke to the Spanish for their treatment of these poor people. Her message was one of hope and compassion. Since then, many miracles have been credited to our Lady of Guadalupe. She is the patron saint of Mexico and honored throughout the world.

Unscramble the following words from the story above and put them in the puzzle.

| | | |
|---|---|---|
| mltia | unaj | godie |
| uchrhc | ryam | gnis |
| sseor | bkreue | epoh |

\_\_\_\_ \_\_\_\_ G \_\_\_\_

\_\_\_\_ \_\_\_\_ U \_\_\_\_ \_\_\_\_ \_\_\_\_

\_\_\_\_ \_\_\_\_ A \_\_\_\_

\_\_\_\_ D \_\_\_\_ \_\_\_\_ \_\_\_\_

\_\_\_\_ A \_\_\_\_

\_\_\_\_ \_\_\_\_ L \_\_\_\_ \_\_\_\_

\_\_\_\_ \_\_\_\_ \_\_\_\_ U \_\_\_\_ \_\_\_\_

\_\_\_\_ \_\_\_\_ P \_\_\_\_

\_\_\_\_ \_\_\_\_ E \_\_\_\_

# Names for Jesus
## Christmas

Name_____

When the angel Gabriel first announced to Mary that she was to have a son, he told her she should name him Jesus, which she did (see Luke 1:31). Every Christian throughout the world recognizes the name Jesus and knows that he is the son of God. Yet Jesus is also known by many other names.

Read each of these Scripture verses and list the name for Jesus found in that verse. Then circle all the names in the Word Search puzzle below.

Matthew 1:16   ___ ___ ___ ___ ___ ___

Matthew 1:23   ___ ___ ___ ___ ___ ___ ___ ___

Matthew 2:23   ___ ___ ___ ___ ___ ___ ___ ___

Luke 1:76   ___ ___ ___ ___ ___ ___ ___ ___

Luke 2:11   ___ ___ ___ ___ ___ ___

Mark 1:11   ___ ___ ___ ___ ___ ___ ___

John 1:1   ___ ___ ___ ___

John 1:29   ___ ___ ___ ___    ___ ___    ___ ___ ___

John 1:38   ___ ___ ___ ___ ___ ___ ___

John 6:35   ___ ___ ___ ___ ___

John 8:12   ___ ___ ___ ___ ___

John 10:11   ___ ___ ___ ___ ___ ___ ___ ___ ___

John 15:1   ___ ___ ___ ___

Revelations 19:16   ___ ___ ___ ___

```
B E L O T D E M S W S O
T E H P I B R E A D H D
R M L R N E N S V R E O
E M M O I I C S I O P G
L A T P V T D I O E H F
H N E H T E U K L A E O
F U N E J A D E I P R B
B E Y T V C W S G T D M
E L A L E H S E H F E A
L I N E D E W A T E H L
O N A S M R S K V A P E
N A Z O R E A N I I W H
P R O P S T E G N N O F
I E P H E R D S W O R R
E A K I N K I N G A D B
```

# Handling Fear
## Holy Family

Name_____

Read Matthew 2:13-15. What is happening?_____

How do you think Joseph felt at this time?_____


Read Matthew 2:16-18. What is happening?_____

How do you think Herod felt at this time? _____


Read Matthew 2:19-23. What is happening? _____

How do you think Joseph felt at this time?_____


In the two frames below, draw a picture or symbol of each man, or list characteristics you think each had.

|  |  |
|---|---|
| Joseph | Herod |

Both Herod and Joseph felt fear, but the cause of their fears was different, and they responded differently. Fear is a feeling and is neither right nor wrong. But the way we respond to fear can be right or wrong. King Herod responded with violence by killing babies. Joseph responded by listening to God, trusting, and being obedient.

Identify one of your own worst fears. On the back of this page, write a few sentences describing how you could handle that fear in a peaceful way. Add a short prayer asking God to help you with your fear.

# Friends and Enemies
## Epiphany

Name_____

On the feast of the Epiphany, we remember when the Magi visited the infant Jesus to pay homage to him and to bring him valuable gifts. They knew he was very special. From the time of Jesus' birth, there were people who loved and honored him. But there were also people who felt threatened by him and wanted to destroy him. God protected Jesus against his enemies through various ways.

Read Matthew 2:1-13. Then complete the crossword below.

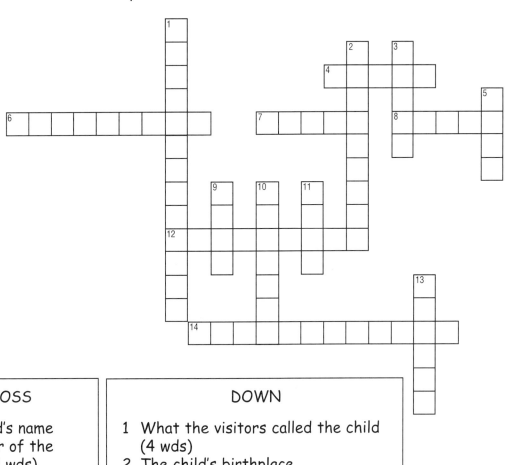

### ACROSS

4 The child's name
6 The ruler of the region (2 wds)
7 Sweet smelling resin
8 The country to which they fled
12 The holy city
14 When burned, sends up aromatic smoke

### DOWN

1 What the visitors called the child (4 wds)
2 The child's birthplace
3 The region of the child's birthplace
5 The visitors saw this rising
9 The child's mother
10 The visitors (2 wds)
11 A precious metal
13 He was warned in a dream

Has anyone ever protected you from harm? Using the back of this page, write a brief story about that event and the person or persons God sent to protect you.

# John's Message
## Baptism of Jesus

Name_____

Shortly after the Epiphany, we celebrate the Baptism of the Lord by John the Baptist. John the Baptist appeared in the wilderness, preaching a baptism of repentance for the forgiveness of sins. John was a messenger sent by God to prepare the way for Jesus.

John proclaimed:

*"The one who is more powerful than I is coming after me; I am not worthy to stoop down and untie the thong of his sandals. I have baptized you with water; but he will baptize you with the Holy Spirit"* (Mark 1-78).

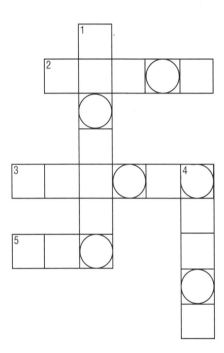

Find five words from John's statement about Jesus that fit in the grid. You must find the right five words and fit them in the correct spots.

When you've accomplished that, use the six letters in the circles to spell the theme for John the Baptist's message to the people.

John the Baptist's Message

___ ___ ___ ___ ___ ___

# In the Spirit of Penance

Name_____

## Ash Wednesday Prayer Service

**Leader:** On this the first day of Lent, our thoughts go to good works, prayer, charitable giving, and sacrifices—all traditional practices for atoning for sin and preparing for the new life of the Resurrection. In the Gospel reading today, we receive very clear directions from Jesus about the proper attitude and disposition to maintain during times of fasting, almsgiving, and sacrifice. We come together now asking for his strength, wisdom, and perseverance as we begin our Lenten journey.

**Reader 1**   *Beware of praying just for show so that others will think you are holy. You will get no reward for such behavior in heaven.*

**All**   Spirit of Piety, help us to pray sincerely and honestly for no other reward than a deeper relationship with God.

**Reader 2**   *Whenever you give gifts to the poor, do not tell others of your generosity so that they will praise you for it.*

**All**   Spirit of Charity, open our hearts to the needs of others and bless our efforts with pure intentions of Christian service.

**Reader 3**   *Whenever you pray, do not be hypocritical. Do not pray only where others may see you, but pray in a private place where God alone is your witness.*

**All**   Spirit of Humility, cleanse our hearts of all traces of deceit, arrogance, and false pride. Fill us with a true spirit of charity, faith, and hope.

**Reader 4**   *When you eliminate or cut back on certain foods, do not look downcast and miserable so that others will feel sorry for you. Keep a pleasant look about you so that no one suspects you are sacrificing.*

**All**   Spirit of Sacrifice, help us persevere without calling attention to any discomfort we may feel. Rather, let us use our hunger and thirst as a reminder of those who struggle for their daily bread.

**Leader**   Jesus, we place these petitions before you today in a spirit of need for your guidance, in a spirit of sorrow for our sins, in a spirit of confidence of your forgiveness, and in a spirit of thankfulness for your everlasting love.

**All**   Amen.

(Based on Matthew 6:1-6, 16-18)

# The Rich Fool
## Lent

Name_____

Lent is a time to think about the values we place on things in our lives. What are the important things? Do we store up the things that make us "rich toward God," or do we save those things that someone else will come take from us?

Read Luke 12:13-21, the story about a man who did not plan ahead. Jesus called him a fool. What do you think was the farmer's real sin? forgetting God? making money? selfishness? hoarding? greed?

Here are two barns. Label one of them "Material Barn." In it, write a list or make a drawing of some possessions you value highly. Label the other barn "Spiritual Barn," and make a list or drawing of qualities or actions you do to become "rich toward God." (Some examples are helping at home, collecting for the poor, attending Mass, praying, or listening to a friend's problems.)

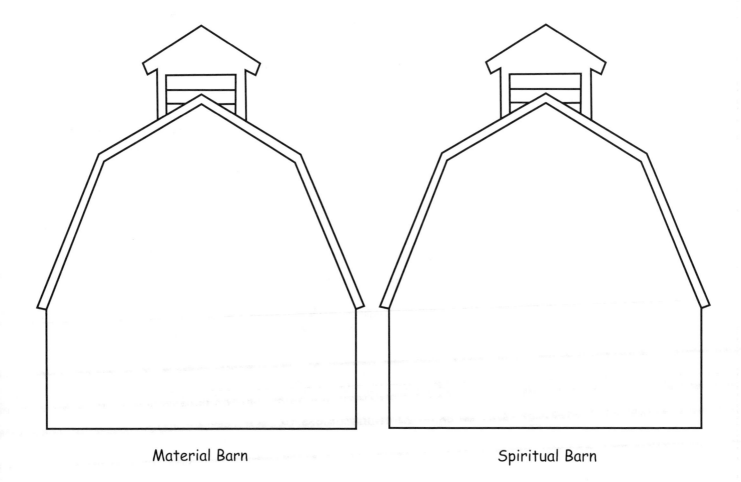

Material Barn                          Spiritual Barn

Reflect or discuss: How might you transfer some things from your material barn to your spiritual barn?

# Spiritual Discipline
## Abstaining

Name_____

*Then Jesus was led up by the Spirit into the wilderness to be tempted by the devil.
He fasted forty days and forty nights, and afterwards he was famished. Matthew 4:1-2*

Abstinence means refraining from eating a certain food for a particular amount of time. For example, Catholics abstain from eating meat on the Fridays of Lent and on Ash Wednesday. In addition, some refrain from eating a favorite food like candy, or soda, or snack foods during Lent.

Fasting means restricting the amount of food you eat. For example, Catholics who fast during Lent restrict their daily intake of food to one full meal per day. They may eat two other meals but those two meals should not total a full meal.

There are different reasons to fast and abstain. Some stem from self interests, for instance, to lose weight or to impress other people with our piety (see Matthew 6:16-18). Other reasons stem from a real desire to grow spiritually, for instance, to increase our awareness of the plight of the hungry or to develop self-discipline.

Abstaining and fasting is not required by the Church for anyone under the age of 15 or over the age of 60. If you have special dietary needs or health concerns, you are also not required to abstain or fast. Never restrict yourself from water or nutritious juices.

Many young people choose to abstain from certain foods during Lent. To explore abstinence a little more, in the first column below, list some reasons why you would want to abstain. In the second column, create an action plan by deciding exactly what you plan to do. For example, if you want to restrict or abstain from a food, list what food it is. Then say how you will do this and for how long.

Reason to Abstain

Action Plan: What, When, How Long?

# Something's Missing
## Palm Sunday

Name_____

There is a key word(s) hidden in each line below, but the key word(s) has one missing letter. Search the indicated Scripture passages to find each word(s). Supply the missing letter, write the key word(s) on the appropriate blank, and also write the missing letter on the lines at the bottom of the page. Note: The missing letter may come at the beginning, middle, or end of the key word(s).

1. Luke 19:29
2. Matthew 21:8
3. Matthew 21:3
4. Luke 19:37
5. Matthew 21:6

6. Luke 19:28
7. Luke 19:38
8. Matthew 21:9
9. Luke 19:39
10. Matthew 21:2

1. ZEHXSPONIXBETHAGEOXEALFWL  _____

2. CPFWKYUUSWBGBRNCHESKBTHUIC  _____

3. AVCEHCGATLMFDOORDIJXIQSCTRA  _____

4. LIAKJVKORTUWJBOUNTOFOLIVES  _____

5. TJVPSLZNVXHZDICIPLESCJCSDK  _____

6. IDGDLBMDEFGJERSALEMXENYFKN  _____

7. BLESSEDISTHEKIGCWHYQBOHNLP  _____

8. NQPJEZYAESONOFAVIDGMOCPZBQ  _____

9. ORPHNHVDPGQFMTECHERMARQOCGB  _____

10. OKBLHOUZDONKEXASTYAXDRMNC  _____

___ ___ ___ ___ ___   ___ ___ ___ ___ ___ ___

# Events of the Days
## Triduum

Name_____

The three days of Passover are called the Paschal Triduum. It begins on Thursday at sunset and ends Sunday at sunset. This is the holiest of times because of the death, burial, and resurrection of Jesus. This shows the great mystery of our faith, that death is always followed by new life.

Below is a mix of exact words and phrases taken from Scripture about events happening to Jesus during this period. Write each word or phrase under the day it happened. If you need help, look up the stories in the Bible. Each day has the same number of events listed.

1. Judas
2. resurrection
3. body of Jesus
4. King of Jews
5. right ear
6. Rabbouni
7. linen cloths
8. crucified

9. Peter denies
10. gardener
11. burial custom
12. cross
13. torches
14. Mary Magdalene
15. Nicodemus
16. cast lots

17. drink the cup
18. saw and believed
19. Pilate
20. spear
21. charcoal fire
22. "I have seen the Lord."
23. Joseph of Arimathea
24. Golgotha

25. "I am he."
26. stone
27. spices
28. Jesus' mother
29. arrested Jesus
30. two angels
31. new tomb
32. pierced

| THURSDAY (beginning at sunset) John 18:1-18 | FRIDAY John 19:16-37 | SATURDAY John 20:38-42 | SUNDAY (until sunset) John 20:1-18 |
|---|---|---|---|
| | | | |

# The Last Supper
## Holy Thursday

Name_____

Read about Jesus' last meal with his disciples before his death: Matthew 26:17-30.

Jesus and his disciples were celebrating the Jewish Passover. Jesus took the symbols of the Passover and gave them new meanings, pointing to his own coming death and resurrection.

In the left column is a list of words from the Jewish Passover and in the right column are words relating to the Last Supper. Draw lines between related phrases.  If you need help, check Exodus 12 for the instructions for the Passover meal.

| Jewish Passover | The Lord's Supper |
|---|---|
| Passover | Body of Jesus |
| Saved from slavery | Blood of Jesus |
| Blood of lamb | Last Supper |
| Exodus 12 | Saved from sin |
| Slavery to freedom | Matthew 26:17-30 |
| Unleavened bread | Crucifixion of Jesus |
| Sacrifice of lamb | Death to new life |

**Complete the following sentences:**

Today the celebration of the Lord's Supper is called ___ ___ ___ ___ ___ ___ ___ ___ ___.

The person who presides is a ___ ___ ___ ___ ___ ___.

The congregation shares the ___ ___ ___ ___ and ___ ___ ___ ___ ___ of Christ.

The people together proclaim the great mystery of faith:

Christ has ___ ___ ___ ___,

Christ is ___ ___ ___ ___ ___,

Christ will ___ ___ ___ ___ ___   ___ ___ ___ ___ ___.

# Why, God?
## Good Friday

James never forgot a lesson he learned when he was ten years old. His teacher, Mr. Frederick, had a two-year-old son who died of leukemia. James really didn't know how to express his feelings, but after class he stayed a minute and simply said, "I'm sorry, Mr. Frederick."

Mr. Frederick replied, "Thanks, James. God must understand how I feel. You see, God lost a son too."

Mr. Frederick's loss helped him understand the meaning of crucifixion. He knew that whatever pain and sorrow we might feel in our lives, God understands.

> *For God so loved the world*
> *that he gave his only Son,*
> *so that everyone who believes in him*
> *may not perish*
> *but may have eternal life.*
> John 3:16

What is the greatest darkness you can imagine? (Examples: doubt, worry, addiction, divorce of parents, loss of love, death of pet, natural disaster.)

_____

What is the greatest darkness you ever experienced yourself?

_____

Did you feel God's presence with you during your time of darkness? Or, if not, upon reflection at a later time, did you see how God was present with you? Explain.

_____

_____

Draw a symbol or picture of
your dark time. If you think
God helped you, try to indicate
how. If you need more room,
use the back of this page.

# Dying and Rising with Christ
## Easter Vigil

Name_____

The Saturday night Easter Vigil recalls the passing from death to new life through resurrection. This happened to Jesus and continues to happen to us. It occurs at both our birth and our death, but also in many small ways in our daily life—something ends so that we can begin another stage of life or growth. We don't always know what transitions will bring.

**Haley passed through junior high and
 went to high school.
Antonio gave up track in order to play baseball.
Kevin used to drive too fast, but after running
 off the road, he vowed to drive carefully.
Robert quit teasing Olivia when he realized how
 much it hurt her feelings.
Jasmine moved to a new town.**

Identify an ordinary time when you "died" to
something and then found "new life."

_____

_____

This passing from death to life is ritualized at the Easter Vigil through baptism. All the people there are invited to renew their baptismal vows.

Read Romans 6:3-4

What idea in this passage from Romans is new to you?

_____

How does this explanation of baptism make you feel?

_____

To what do you wish to die at this point in your life?

_____

To what do you want God to raise you?

_____

# Our Easter Hope
## Easter

Name_____

> For there is hope for a tree,
> if it is cut down, that it will sprout again,
> and that its shoots will not cease.
>
> Though its root grows old in the earth,
> and its stump dies in the ground,
> yet at the scent of water it will bud
> and put forth branches like a
> young plant.
>
> But mortals die, and are laid low;
> humans expire, and where are they?
>
> Job 14:7-10

Our hope in resurrection is based on a mystery. We look around us for symbols to show the truth of it. "If it happens to trees, will it happen to us?" asks the writer of Job. Seeds, flower bulbs, and eggs are also symbols of new life from the world of nature.

The creatures of God's earth—animals, insects, and birds—also provide symbols of resurrection. Think about the events of new life that happen within everyday life, plus resurrection at the end of life. Then think about symbols from nature.

Write the name of an animal, insect, bird, plant, etc., which best symbolizes resurrection for

you. _____

What quality of the example you chose reminds you of resurrection?

_____

How does the resurrection of Jesus add hope to our belief in new life?

_____

On the back side of this paper, draw a picture or symbol of a part of nature that you think teaches about resurrection.

# Forty Days Later
## Ascension

Name_____

Read the story of Jesus' ascension into heaven in Acts 1:6-11. Its message is that Jesus is now Lord over all, raised by God above all earthly authority.

Then read Ephesians 1:17-23, Paul's description of Jesus' reign from heaven.

What a contrast in these two readings compared to Jesus' experiences during Holy Week!

When working this puzzle, keep in mind that the answers all reflect the contrasting feelings or events between the Holy Week stories and the Ascension stories.

### Across
2. Christ is its head
6. Uncovered
8. An expert
10. Make fun of
11. Deceive
14. Killed on a cross
15. Awareness of something new
16. Taunt and tease cruelly
17. Understanding
18. Knowledge

### Down
1. Prickly nodes
3. Strength
4. Lead
5. Completeness
7. Something you get from someone else
9. A state of great honor
12. Fearful
13. Desire or yearn

# Spiritgram
## Pentecost

Name_____

After Jesus had gone back to the Father, the disciples gathered together in fear. Being a follower of Christ was not a popular political position, and in addition the disciples were supposed to go out and preach the Good News to everyone. How could they overcome their fear?

Jesus had promised to send his Spirit but the disciples didn't know what to expect or how this would happen. Suddenly, as they waited together, a noise came from the sky like a strong wind. Tongues as of fire appeared over each of them, and they were filled with the Spirit's gifts of wisdom, understanding, right judgment, courage, knowledge, piety, and fear of the Lord. These are the same gifts we receive at Confirmation.

A Spiritgram is a reminder of the Spirit of God that came on the wind that first Pentecost.

To make a Spiritgram, you will need:
• a brown grocery bag
• scissors
• raffia or jute string
• permanent markers
• paper punch

Directions
1. Cut out the pattern strip on this page.
2. Trace the pattern strip onto a brown grocery sack and cut it out.
3. Punch a hole in the top of the paper strip as indicated.
4. Fold the top down about three-quarters of an inch.
5. Tie a string loop through the hole.
6. On one side of the strip, draw a symbol of fire.
7. On the other side, write the gifts of the Spirit.
8. Hang the Spiritgram on a tree branch in your yard, garden, or woods.

*Raw and incomplete when just written, the Spiritgram needs the strong wind, the rain, and sun. It will gradually fade and its edges will get ragged. Leave it until it becomes a part of nature just as the Spirit's gifts become a part of you.*

# Simeon Says

Name_____

## Presentation of the Lord

Read about Jesus' visit to the Temple in Luke 2:22-38. Fill in the missing letters in this short version of the Bible story. Then transfer the number letters to the spaces below to learn what Simeon predicted about Jesus.

M___ ___ ___ and J___ ___ ___ ___ h brou___h___ the bab___ J___ sus
  11 27 28      14 23 9 36      16 12      29  7

to the ___ emp___e to prese___t ___ ___m to ___od.
     5     1      15  4 2    3

S___m___on, a ri___hteous man, ___i___ed in J___ ___ ___ sa___em
13 17    24      10 8    22 6 31   25

and was t___ ___d by the Holy Sp___rit he would see the Mes___ ___ah
     26 37          20            40 39

before he di___d.
     38

When he saw Jesus, he dec___ a___ed that he c___u___d ___ ___w
             21  41      35 44  18 30

depa___ ___ in ___ ___ ___c___ .
32 19    33 34 42 43

Simeon declared that Jesus would become, "A ___ ___ ___ ___ ___ for
                         1  2  3  4  5

___ ___ ___ ___ ___ ___ ___ ___ ___ ___ to the ___ ___ ___ ___ ___ ___ ___ ___
6 7 8 9 10 11 12 13 14 15      16 17 18 19 20 21 22 23

and for ___ ___ ___ ___ ___ to ___ ___ ___ ___ ___ ___ ___ ___ ___ ___
       24 25 26 27 28    29 30 31 32    33 34 35 36 37 38

___ ___ ___ ___ ___ ___ ."
39 40 41 42 43 44

# Assumption of Mary
## August 15

Name_____

The feast of the Assumption celebrates Mary's entrance into heaven. She was a human person and is now totally redeemed and living with her son, Jesus, enjoying his glory and majesty. She is the Queen of Heaven.

Because Mary was human just as we are, we see that even if we suffer trials and sorrows in this world, we can attain eternal happiness and peace in heaven. The feast of the Assumption of Mary is a day to celebrate both the earthly life that Mary led and the eternal life she now enjoys.

### A Poem to Honor Mary

A cinquain is a kind of poem with five lines. Follow the pattern for the poem and write your own cinquain in honor of Mary. If you need to jog your memory about Mary, read Luke 1:26-56.

1. The first line is a noun—the subject of the poem (Mary).
2. The second line is two adjectives that describe the subject.
3. The third line is three verbs that relate to the subject.
4. The fourth line is a four-word descriptive phrase about the subject.
5. The fifth line is another noun that is a synonym for the subject.

## MARY

_____    _____

_____    _____    _____

_____    _____    _____

_____

# All Saints Day
## November 1

Name_____

On this day, we remember and honor all men and women whose lives have modeled the commandment to love God and others. They are an inspiration for our own journeys. The first saints familiar to many of us are those who lived when Jesus did. Match these saints with the correct clues. If you don't know an answer, look it up in the Scripture reference. (Be careful, there are two more names than you need!)

1. He denied Jesus three times. (John 18:27)

2. He persecuted Christians before his conversion. (Acts 9:1)

3. The name Peter's parents gave him.  (Mt 4:18)

4. Zebedee was their father. (Mt 4:21)

5. Sisters who were Jesus' friends (John 11:5)

6. He was called "the twin." (John 11:16)

7. Peter's brother (Matthew 4:18)

8. She was married to Zechariah and related to Jesus.

   (Luke 1:5,36)

9. He prepared people for Jesus' coming. (Matthew 3:1-3)

10. He was stoned to death. (Acts 7:59)

11. He helped Jesus carry his cross. (Mark 15:21)

12. She stood beneath the cross with Jesus' mother.

   (John 19:25)

a. Andrew

b. Martha and Mary

c. James and John

d. Thomas

e. John the Baptist

f. Mary

g. Timothy

h.  Mary Magdalene

i. Simon of Cyrene

j. Stephen

k. Paul

l. Elizabeth

m. Simon

n. Peter

Answers

1. ____   5. ____   9. ____

2. ____   6. ____   10. ____

3. ____   7. ____   11. ____

4. ____   8. ____   12. ____

# The Year Ends
## Christ the King

Name_____

Read Matthew 25:31-46 about how our king will judge us. Then answer these questions. When you are finished, cut out the bookmark and use it in your Bible.

1. Who are the three main characters [or groups of characters] in

the story? _____

_____

_____

2. Whom does each of these characters represent?

_____

_____

_____

3. Identify two of the characters who get a big surprise, and tell why they are surprised.

_____

_____

4. List acts of mercy mentioned in this Scripture. Remember that these represent basic human needs, and any act of kindness counts.

_____

_____

_____

_____

5. Jesus is the King in the story, but Jesus is also present with us in what group of people? _____

6. Identify one kind thing you did for someone without really thinking about it. _____

7. Identify one good thing you might have done for someone but neglected to do. _____

Blessed are the merciful, for they will receive mercy.
Matthew 5:7

Jesus, I know you want me to show mercy toward people less fortunate than I. My intentions are good, but sometimes I get busy and don't notice. Help me to recognize those who need my kindness. Then please help me to follow through with loving acts. Amen.

# Notes to Teacher

## How We Celebrate Our Year
1. Pentecost; 2. Epiphany; 3. Advent; 4. Easter Vigil; 5. Holy Thursday; 6. Palm Sunday; 7. Easter; 8. All Saints Day; 9. Ash Wednesday; 10. Good Friday.

## Our Lady of Guadalupe
Answers: sign; church; Juan; Diego; Mary; tilma; rebuke; hope; roses

## Names for Jesus
Messiah
Emmanuel
Nazorean
Prophet
Savior
Beloved
Word
Lamb of God
Teacher
Bread
Light
Shepherd
Vine
King

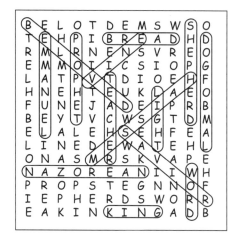

## Friends and Enemies
**Across:** 4=Jesus; 6=King Herod; 7=myrrh; 8=Egypt; 12=Jerusalem; 14=frankincense.
**Down:** 1=King of the Jews; 2=Bethlehem; 3=Judea; 5=star; 9=Mary; 10=Wise Men; 11=gold; 13=Joseph

## John's Message
Across: 2=water; 3=spirit; 5=one
Down: 1=Baptize; 4=thong
Message: REPENT

## Something's Missing
1. Bethphage; 2. branches; 3. Lord; 4. Mount of Olives; 5. disciples; 6. Jerusalem; 7. Blessed is the King; 8. Son of David; 9. teacher; 10. donkey
PALM SUNDAY

## Events of the Days
Thursday: 1, 13, 25, 5, 17, 29, 9, 21
Friday: 12, 24, 4, 16, 28, 8, 20, 32
Saturday: 23, 3, 15, 27, 7, 19, 31, 11
Sunday: 2, 14, 26, 6, 18, 30, 10, 22

## The Last Supper
Passover/Last Supper
Saved from slavery/Saved from sin
Blood of lamb/Blood of Jesus
Exodus 12/Matthew 26:17-30
Slavery to freedom/Death to new life
Unleavened bread/Body of Jesus
Sacrifice of lamb/Crucifixion of Jesus
Eucharist; priest; body/blood; died, risen, come again.

## Forty Days Later
### Across
2. Church; 6. stripped; 8. authority; 10. ridicule; 11. betray; 14. crucified; 15. revelation; 16. mock; 17. enlightenment; 18. wisdom.
### Down
1. thorns; 3. power; 4. rule; 5. fullness; 7. inheritance; 9. glory; 12. afraid; 13. hope.

## Simeon Says
"A light for revelation to the Gentiles and for glory to your people Israel" (Luke 2:32).

## All Saints Day
| | | |
|---|---|---|
| 1. n | 5. b | 9. e |
| 2. k | 6. d | 10. j |
| 3. m | 7. a | 11. i |
| 4. c | 8. l | 12. h |

## The Year Ends
1. King, sheep, goats
2. King=Jesus; sheep=people who do acts of mercy; goats=people who neglect to do acts of mercy
3. sheep: didn't know they were being righteous; goats: thought they were being righteous. (Not bad people but simply neglected to do good.)
4. fed the hungry; gave drink to thirsty; welcomed strangers; visited people in prison
5. the poor or the homeless or the imprisoned